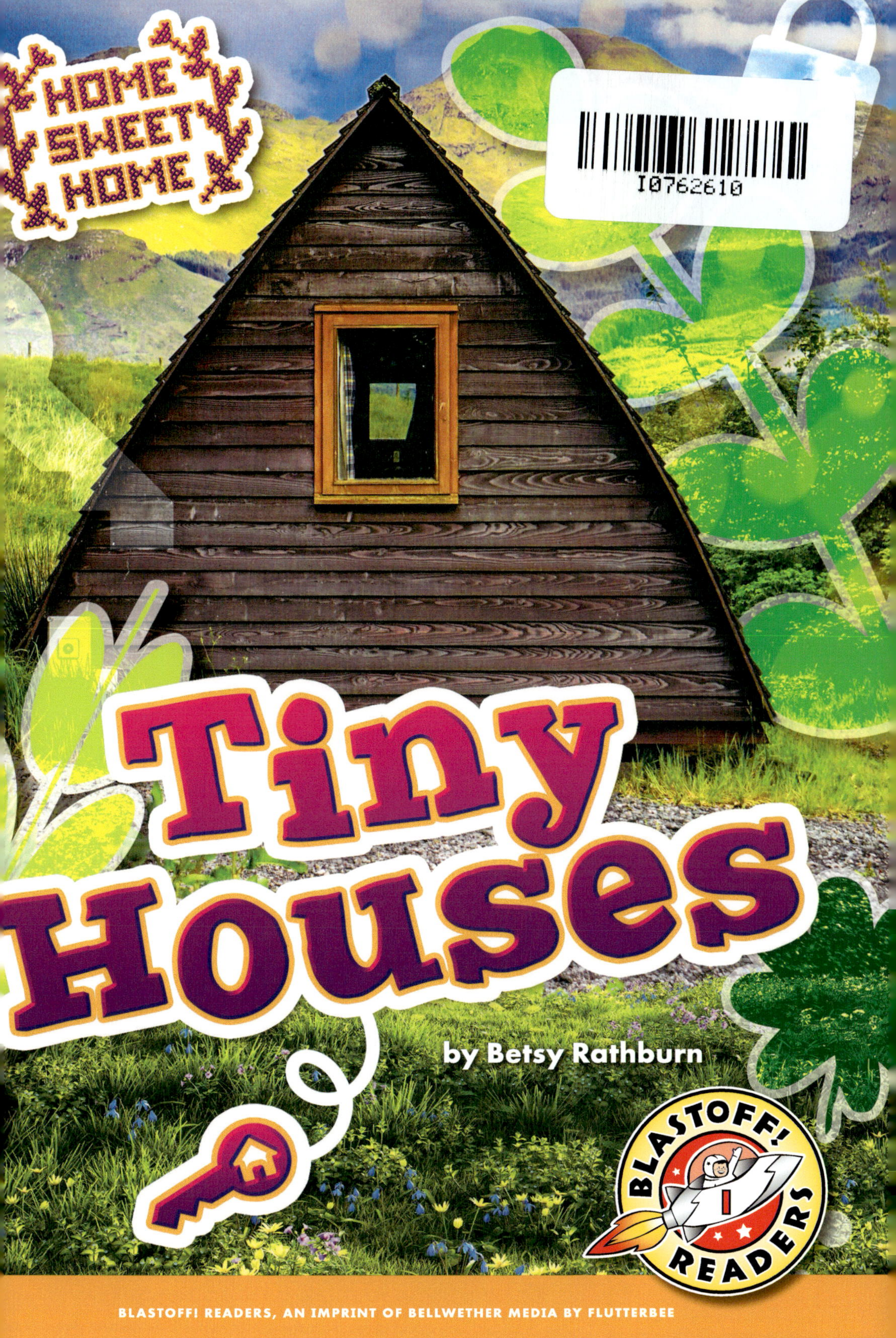
HOME
SWEET
HOME
I0762610
Tiny
Houses
by Betsy Rathburn
BLASTOFF!
1
READERS
BLASTOFF! READERS, AN IMPRINT OF BELLWETHER MEDIA BY FLUTTERBEE

Blastoff! Readers are carefully developed by literacy experts to build reading stamina and move students toward fluency by combining standards-based content with developmentally appropriate text.

Level 1 provides the most support through repetition of high-frequency words, light text, predictable sentence patterns, and strong visual support.

Level 2 offers early readers a bit more challenge through varied sentences, increased text load, and text-supportive special features.

Level 3 advances early-fluent readers toward fluency through increased text load, less reliance on photos, advancing concepts, longer sentences, and more complex special features.

★ **Blastoff! Universe**

Reading Level

Grade K

Grades 1–3

Grade 4

This edition first published in 2027 by Bellwether Media, Inc.

Library of Congress Cataloging-in-Publication Data

Names: Rathburn, Betsy author
Title: Tiny houses / by Betsy Rathburn.
Description: Blastoff! readers. | Minneapolis, Minnesota : Bellwether Media, Inc, 2027. | Includes bibliographical references and index. | Audience: Ages 5-8 | Audience: Grades 2-3 | Summary: "Developed by literacy experts for students in kindergarten through grade three, this book introduces tiny houses to young readers through leveled text and related photos"– Provided by publisher.
Identifiers: LCCN 2026011559 (print) | LCCN 2026011560 (ebook) | ISBN 9798898800291 library binding | ISBN 9798898802820 paperback | ISBN 9798898801533 ebook
Subjects: LCSH: Tiny houses
Classification: LCC NA7533 .R38 2027 (print) | LCC NA7533 (ebook)
LC record available at https://lccn.loc.gov/2026011559
LC ebook record available at https://lccn.loc.gov/2026011560

Editor: Rebecca Sabelko Designer: Andrea Schneider

Printed in the United States of America, North Mankato, MN.

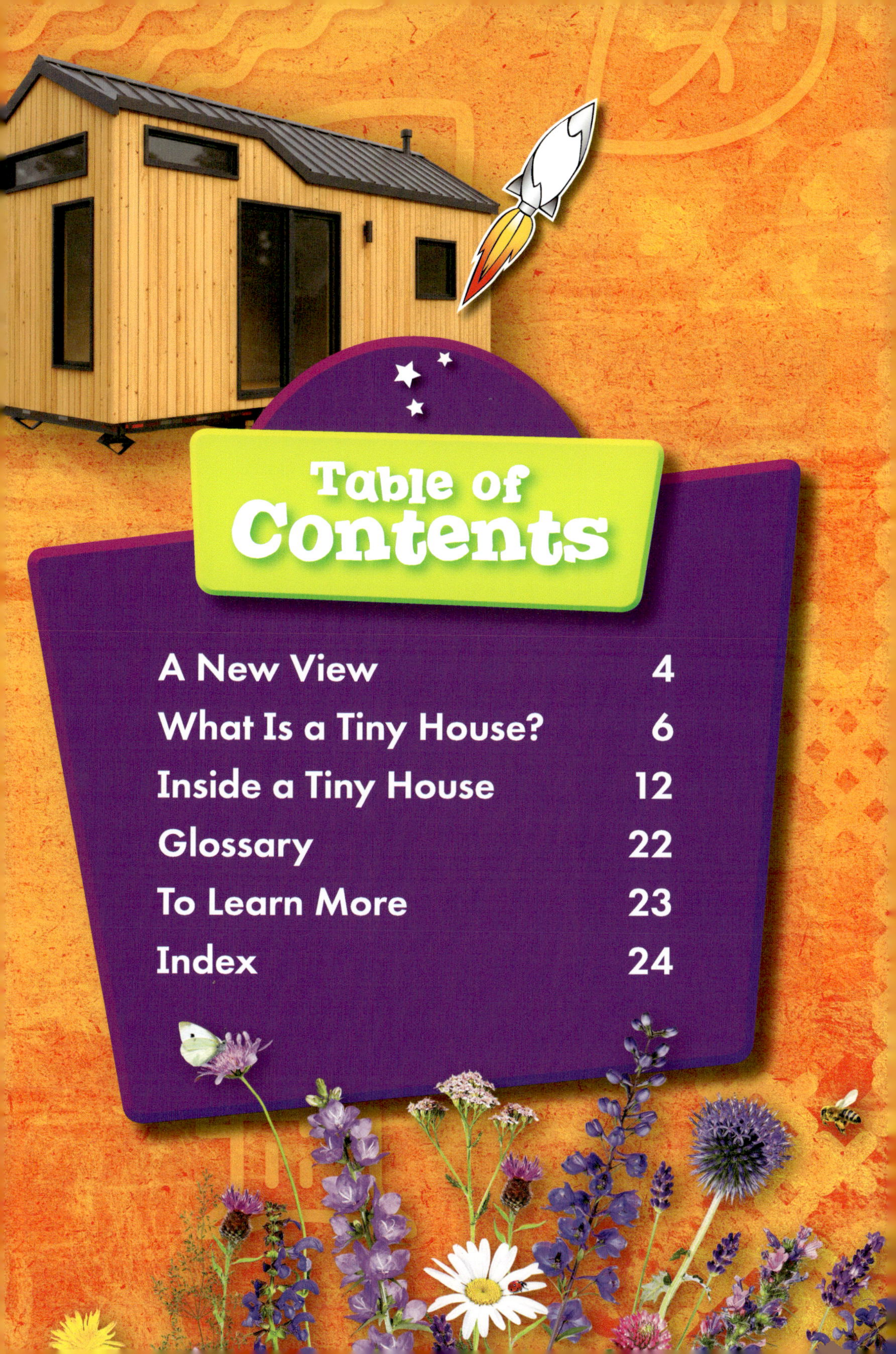

Table of Contents

A New View

We are moving. Our tiny house moves with us. Here is our new yard!

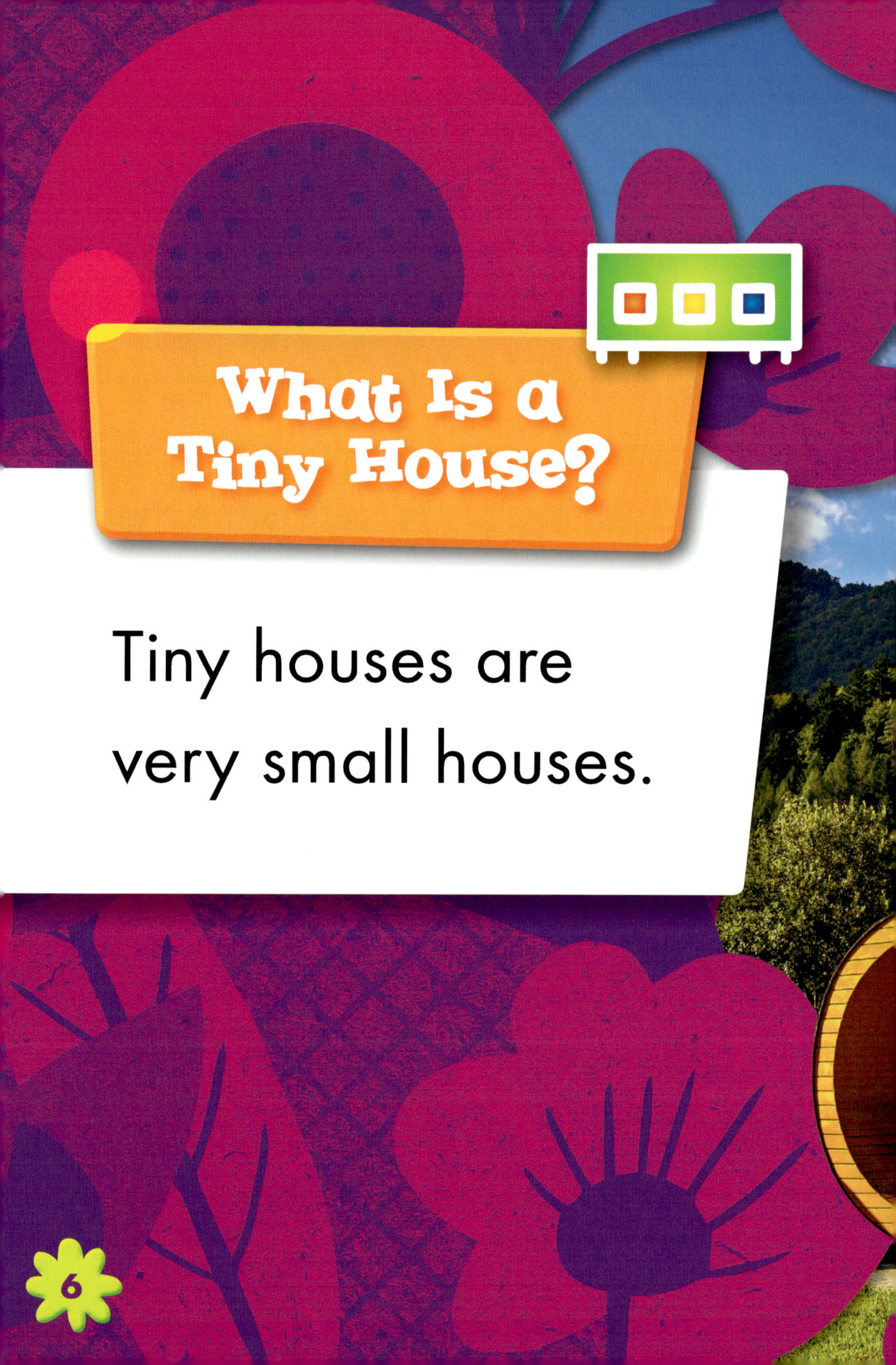

What Is a Tiny House?

Tiny houses are very small houses.

Size of a Tiny House
2 school buses
1 tiny house

Some tiny houses stay in one place.

Others can be moved with **trailers**.

trailer

Inside a Tiny House

A tiny house is like a regular house. It has windows, a door, and a roof.

roof
door
window

It has a kitchen
and a bathroom.
It may have small
appliances.

appliance
kitchen

Some tiny houses have one open room. Small **furniture** folds away for more space.

furniture

Other tiny houses have several rooms. Some have a **loft**. This one has two **stories**!

stories
Parts of a Tiny House
bathroom
loft
kitchen

Tiny houses are small. But they make cozy homes!

Glossary

appliances

tools or machines that have special uses

furniture

items such as chairs and tables that make rooms ready to use

loft

an upper floor that overlooks the main living space in a house

stories

floors in a building

trailers

the back part of a truck that carries loads

To Learn More

AT THE LIBRARY

Dickmann, Nancy. *Wild Wheels. RVs.* North Mankato, Minn.: Capstone Press, 2020.

Lawrence, Ellen. *Homes Around the World.* Minneapolis, Minn.: Ruby Tuesday Books, 2025.

Jones, Christianne. *Measuring at Home.* North Mankato, Minn.: Pebble, 2022.

ON THE WEB

FACTSURFER

Factsurfer.com gives you a safe, fun way to find more information.

1. Go to www.factsurfer.com.
2. Enter "tiny houses" into the search box and click 🔍.
3. Select your book cover to see a list of related content.

Index

The images in this book are reproduced through the courtesy of: Dora Dorja, front cover; Anna, p. 3 (house); Marina Lohrbach, p. 3 (flowers); Tony Anderson/ Getty Images, pp. 4-5; Pazyuk, pp. 6-7; anjokan, pp. 8-9; inrainbows, pp. 10-11; Eco Tiny House, p. 11 (trailer); INTREEGUE Photography, pp. 12-13; Maria Korneeva/ Getty Images, pp. 14-15; ppa5, p. 15 (appliance); Michaela Komi, pp. 16-17; imaginima, pp. 18-19; panu101, p. 19 (parts); emirhankaramuk, p. 19 (bathroom); Bigc Studio, pp. 20-21; Pixel-Shot, p. 22 (appliances); FollowTheFlow, p. 22 (furniture); Victor zastol'skiy, p. 22 (loft); bmak, p. 22 (stories); AscentXmedia, p. 22 (trailers).